Michael Gannon's History of Florida in Forty Minutes

UNIVERSITY PRESS OF FLORIDA

Florida A&M University, Tallahassee
Florida Atlantic University, Boca Raton
Florida Gulf Coast University, Ft. Myers
Florida International University, Miami
Florida State University, Tallahassee
University of Central Florida, Orlando
University of Florida, Gainesville
University of North Florida, Jacksonville
University of South Florida, Tampa
University of West Florida, Pensacola

Michael Gannon's

History of

FLO

University Press of Florida

Gainesville · Tallahassee · Tampa · Boca Raton

Pensacola · Orlando · Miami · Jacksonville · Ft. Myers

RIDA

IN **40** Minutes

Michael Gannon

12 11 10 09 08 07   6 5 4 3 2 1

The following permissions relate to the music on the companion CD:
"Recuerdos de la Alhambra," performed by Julian Bream. Courtesy of RCA
records, by arrangement with Sony BMG Entertainment.
Permission granted by Bobby Hicks, writer and performer of the song "I'm
Florida," recording from the Will McLean Folk Festival on March 13, 1999.

Library of Congress Cataloging-in-Publication Data
Gannon, Michael, 1927-
Michael Gannon's history of Florida in forty minutes / Michael Gannon.
p. cm.
"Includes both an audio compact disk and accompanying illustrated book
presenting a conversational view of Florida history as seen by preeminent
state historian Michael Gannon; the speech itself is an overview of the
state's entire history, spanning the time from its original inhabitants to
the 2005 hurricane season, and is structured as a description of ten main
watershed periods"—Pub. info.
ISBN-13: 978-0-8130-3068-5 (alk. paper)
1. Florida—History. I. Title. II. Title: History of Florida in forty minutes.
F311.G345   2007
975.9—dc22   2006030872

The University Press of Florida is the scholarly publishing agency for the
State University System of Florida, comprising Florida A&M University,
Florida Atlantic University, Florida Gulf Coast University, Florida Inter-
national University, Florida State University, University of Central Florida,
University of Florida, University of North Florida, University of South
Florida, and University of West Florida.

University Press of Florida
15 Northwest 15th Street
Gainesville, FL 32611-2079
http://www.upf.com

Acknowledgments

For many years, I have given this talk, constantly updated, to audiences throughout the State of Florida. To each one I have said that, if you have had a bad experience with history as a subject in school, *relax*, the pain this time will only last 40 minutes!

Year after year, Ms. Wendy Abbeger, director of Leadership Florida, and her co-worker Gayle Webb, have asked me to give this talk, in one or another of its changing forms, to each annual statewide leadership class. I have always been eager to do so, because, quoting the acclaimed paleontologist Teilhard de Chardin: "Everything is the sum of the past, and nothing is understandable except through its history."

The publication of this talk is owed to initiatives taken by Meredith Morris-Babb, director, and John Byram, editor-in-chief, of the University Press of Florida. I thank them for their expressions of confidence. Gillian Hillis edited the manuscript. Larry Leshan supervised the design and illustrations. Bill Beckett, program director of WUFT-FM, in Gainesville, directed my reading of the text and produced the audio format.

The History of Florida in Forty Minutes

~~~~~~

Probably it would come as a surprise to most of the eighteen million residents of Florida to learn that this peninsula and Panhandle have the longest recorded history of any of the American states. In the minds of many newcomers, Florida has no meaningful history prior to the Second World War and the beginning of our current population boom. It must have been all trackless wilderness before that date, goes a common assumption.

But other Floridians, long-time residents, recall that the state went through a major real estate boom (and bust) in the early and mid-1920s. And the now relatively few old families that go back many generations can tell us that Florida became a state in 1845, and that five thousand of her sons gave their lives in what was called locally "The War Between the States."

Still other Floridians, more far-reaching in their knowledge, because of what they learned from books and journal articles, remember that Florida was first discovered, settled, and governed by Spain—sometime way back when?

To put a fine point on it, the peninsula was discovered by record-writing Europeans early in the sixteenth century, first, it is commonly believed, in 1513 by the Spaniard Juan Ponce de León, who had sailed with Christopher Columbus twenty-one years before. More than three centuries of sunrises and sunsets lay between the first and final appearances of the Spanish flag in Florida, and it will be the twenty-second century before the same can be said about the flag of the United States.

Those numbers from our Spanish past alone give an indication how far we can trace Florida's story in the written record.

Let me take you on a rapid cruise through Florida's centuries. If asked to name the *ten* key populations, periods, groups of periods, or factors that shaped Florida's history, I would list the following.

1

The first people who discovered Florida, the **original inhabitants**, who entered the state some twelve thousand years ago to become Florida's pioneer land developers. These native people had no written language of their own, but they left their history underground in the form of artifacts such as pottery and stone tools, now being recovered by archaeologists.

From the Spaniards and the French, who first studied the native populations four and a half centuries ago, we know their national groupings by name, such as the Panzacola, Chatot, and Apalachicola in the northwest; the Apalachee around present-day Tallahassee; the Timucua in the northern half of the peninsula; the Calusa in the southwest; the Tequesta at Biscayne Bay; and the Matecumbe in the Keys.

The better-known Seminole do not appear until very late in the Florida story. Originally Lower Creeks from the Georgia-Alabama line, the Seminole first entered Florida during the early 1700s, just two and three-quarter centuries ago.

Many of north Florida's original natives were a settled agricultural people by the time of first contact with Europeans. Their principal crop was maize, or corn. But they also planted beans, squashes, and pumpkins. Along the seashores and estuaries they consumed fish, oysters, and clams, and throughout the peninsula they hunted animals and foraged for wild plants. They wore a minimum of clothing, the men a deerskin breechcloth, the women a short skirt made from Spanish moss. Their god was the sun.

At first contact they numbered, in all, about three hundred and fifty thousand persons, the largest number being Timucuan. Today the locations of their tribal chiefdoms are familiar to Florida scholars, as are their shell middens and burial mounds, their arrowheads and wooden masks, in ancient fields where ghostly campfires seem still to burn.

English artist and cartographer John White executed this sixteenth-century drawing of an original Florida native belonging to the Timucua nation, who occupied the northern half of the Florida peninsula. The Timucua men wore their hair trussed up in the shape of a bun, adorned their bodies with tattoos, and wore only a deerskin breechcloth. They were skilled archers.

In an engraving published by Theodore de Bry in 1591, Timucua natives are shown giving homage to the burial mound of a chief. In the upper left corner the engraving depicts part of a typical Timucua village, circular in form, with huts surrounded by tree trunks.

2

I would name the **first Spanish settlers**. Following a half century of explorations of Florida by five Spanish expeditions, and one brief French encampment, a permanent European settlement was finally established in 1565, at the northeast corner of the peninsula. Its founder was one of Spain's most successful admirals, the Asturian Pedro Menéndez de Avilés. Because his fleet had first sighted Florida's shoreline on the feast day of Saint Augustine, Menéndez gave that saint's name to his colonial development.

Five hundred soldiers, two hundred sailors, and one hundred farmers and craftsmen, some with wives and children, made up the list of settlers whose city, fort, and Christian parish took shape forty-two years before the English settled Jamestown in Virginia, and fifty-five years before the Pilgrims came to Plymouth in Massachusetts. Or, as I like to say, by the time the Pilgrims came to Plymouth, St. Augustine was up for urban renewal.

Shortly after the Spaniards' landing, French forces came by sea to destroy the infant settlement, but were shipwrecked south of St. Augustine by a storm. Menéndez decided that he had no choice but to kill many of the French survivors because he had no ships on which to send them away, no food to give them, and no weapons sufficient to guard them. It being a time of sectarian strife, Menéndez also justified his action as an elimination of Protestant "heretics" who might "rightly" be put to the sword.

Besides being the oldest city in what is now the United States, St. Augustine also became the site of our country's first church, first hospital, first school, first court of law, first market, and first city plan. During her nearly two and a half centuries under Spanish rule, St. Augustine never achieved the grandeur of Spanish cities in Mexico and Peru. She was always a bare subsistence garrison town. But no city in the Spanish Americas was more loyal to the Spanish crown. The kings and queens of Spain knew this outpost as *la siempre fiel ciudad de San Agustín*—"the always faithful city of Saint Augustine."

Juan Ponce de León, native of Valladolid in Spain (ca. 1460–1521), is believed to have been the first European discoverer of the peninsula, in 1513. He named his discovery, which he thought was an island, La Florida—the Flowery Land. On a second voyage to Florida in 1521 he suffered a fatal Indian arrow wound while attempting to build a settlement on the lower Gulf coast.

The founder of the first permanent and continuously occupied European settlement in Florida was the Spanish admiral Pedro Menéndez de Avilés (1519–1574). The founding date was September 8, 1565. His city, which Menéndez named St. Augustine, still keeps her stately vigil of over 440 years.

This map of Florida was drawn by the French artist and cartographer Jacques le Moyne de Morgues, possibly as early as 1564. It was not printed until 1591, in Frankfurt. Only one place name would be familiar to modern readers: Cape Canaveral.

3

I would name the **Franciscan missions** to the native Florida populations, begun two centuries before the better known missions of California. Shortly after his founding of St. Augustine, Pedro Menéndez invited the Franciscan Order in Spain to evangelize and educate the native Floridians. The first contingent of gray-robed friars to arrive here established Florida's first mission in north St. Augustine. Named Nombre de Dios, meaning Name of God, that mission would soon be followed by many others along the Atlantic coast and inland.

The friars founded their first mission in the Florida interior near present-day Gainesville, toward the beginning of the seventeenth century, and, by the middle of that century, when they numbered 70 missionaries in 38 churches, they could count 26,000 Christian converts from the Atlantic to the Gulf. The western anchor of the interior mission trail was Mission San Luis de Talimali in today's Tallahassee. Its church has recently been reconstructed on the original foundations.

In general, the friars did not change the locations of the native villages. Nor did they expropriate the native lands. Instead, the missionaries lived among the natives much as Peace Corps volunteers live respectfully within foreign societies today. Their primary mission was to preach the Gospel, celebrate Mass, and administer the sacraments. But they also taught European farming, cattle and hog raising, weaving, music, and, in many instances, reading and writing. Although, as mentioned earlier, the natives had no written language, the friars provided them one, using Spanish consonants and vowels. Here is how the first sentences of the Lord's Prayer sounded in Timucuan:

Heka itimile, numa
hibantema, bisamilenema
abokwanoletahabema;
balunu nanemima
nohobonihabe.

The voices of Florida from long ago.

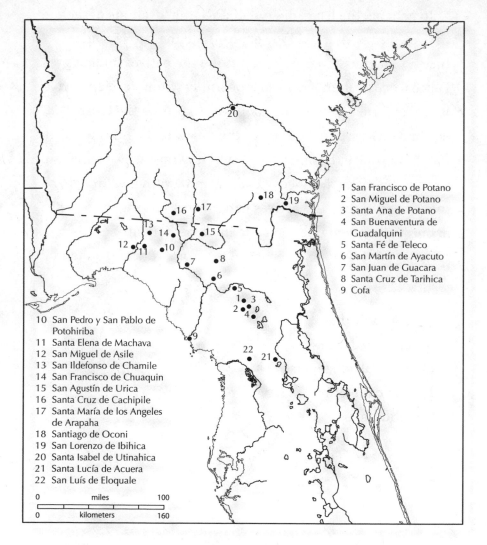

1 San Francisco de Potano
2 San Miguel de Potano
3 Santa Ana de Potano
4 San Buenaventura de Guadalquini
5 Santa Fé de Teleco
6 San Martín de Ayacuto
7 San Juan de Guacara
8 Santa Cruz de Tarihica
9 Cofa

10 San Pedro y San Pablo de Potohiriba
11 Santa Elena de Machava
12 San Miguel de Asile
13 San Ildefonso de Chamile
14 San Francisco de Chuaquin
15 San Agustín de Urica
16 Santa Cruz de Cachipile
17 Santa María de los Angeles de Arapaha
18 Santiago de Oconi
19 San Lorenzo de Ibihica
20 Santa Isabel de Utinahica
21 Santa Lucía de Acuera
22 San Luís de Eloquale

0   miles   100
0   kilometers   160

The Florida Franciscan missions were started two centuries before the better-known missions of the same religious order in California. In this graphic we see the early growth of the interior missions, starting in 1606 with San Francisco de Potano, eight miles northwest of present-day Gainesville, as far as the year 1630.

The western anchor of the cross-Florida mission chain was San Luis (St. Louis) de Talimali, at present-day Tallahassee, founded in 1656. Recently, archaeologists and historians identified the original foundations of the mission church, which, as shown here, has been reconstructed.

4

I would name the **British**, for three reasons. First, in the years 1702–6 British raiders with Indian allies from Carolina destroyed the Florida missions and either killed, enslaved, or forced into exile the Christian converts. The atrocity continues to elude American history textbooks. Second, in 1702 and again in 1740 British forces from Carolina and Georgia besieged St. Augustine and its coquina rock castle, but both times were repulsed. And, third, by virtue of the Treaty of Paris in 1763 that ended the French and Indian War, the British came into possession of Florida and ruled it for the next twenty-one years.

Because the Florida that Britain inherited stretched as far west as the Mississippi River, London divided it into two colonies, East Florida, with a capital at St. Augustine, and West Florida, with a capital at Pensacola. Those were the fourteenth and fifteenth British colonies that we never hear about because both remained loyal to King George the Third during the American Revolution.

In the two Floridas the British established our now familiar common law and such governing principles as trial by jury and religious liberty. British landowners introduced large-scale plantation farming, exploiting enslaved Africans as the primary labor force. From New Smyrna in the south to St. Marys River in the north, East Florida planters grew the dye-stuff indigo for export and food crops such as rice and sugar cane. In West Florida the principal products were furs, barrel staves, and naval stores.

The British remodeled and improved many of the buildings that they inherited from the Spaniards. In St. Augustine, for example, the Church of England refurbished the interior of the Catholic parish church and mounted above its entrance a tower and steeple in the same Georgian style one sees today on colonial churches in New England.

Disney World may have its fairy-tale towers, but St. Augustine boasts a *real* castle, the never-conquered Spanish Castillo de San Marcos (Castle of St. Mark). Its four bastions, moat, and drawbridge are clearly seen in this aerial photograph. Twice, in 1702 and 1740, the castle repulsed English siege forces from Carolina and Georgia, respectively.

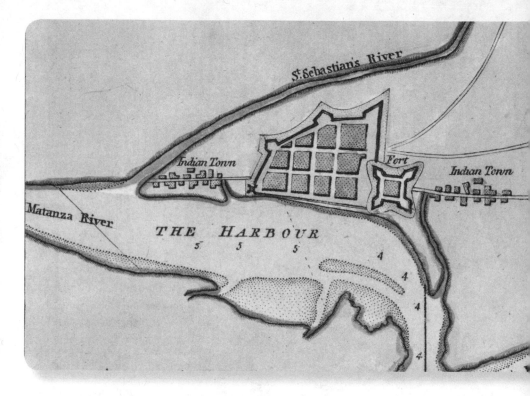

This map by English cartographer Thomas Jefferys
(1699–1775) depicts St. Augustine in 1762. To the north
(right) of the city and castle Jefferys shows the old
mission Nombre de Dios ("Indian Town").

When Florida passed from Spanish to British rule in 1763, London divided the province into two colonies, East Florida with a capital at St. Augustine, and West Florida with a capital at Pensacola. The first governor of West Florida, depicted in this portrait, was a professional naval officer, George Johnstone (1730–1787).

5

I would name together the **Spanish restoration** and **American territorial periods**. Both were times of governmental turmoil. Under the terms of a second Treaty of Paris in 1783 ending the American Revolution, Spain regained her former Florida colony, now much enlarged. She retained the British model of two Floridas, east and west, but her hold on both was shaky all through the thirty-seven-year restoration period.

In the west, immigrants from the infant United States declared independence from Spain and, in support, Washington forcibly annexed all the lands from the Mississippi to the Perdido River, the present western boundary of the State of Florida.

In the east, Spanish lands were so overrun with Yankee adventurers, U.S. armed forces, and freebooting pirates that Spain elected to abandon what was left of the Floridas. On February 22, 1819, her minister to Washington signed a treaty of cession to the United States. In exchange for Florida, the

U.S. government assumed five million dollars of Spanish debts to American citizens. A formal transfer of flags took place in the summer of 1821.

First governor of the new U.S. possession was General Andrew Jackson, of Tennessee. Although he remained in Florida only three months, Jackson began the Americanization of the old Spanish province, establishing counties, courts, and trial by jury. Florida became an official U.S. Territory in 1822. The following year the Indian fields of Tallahassee were selected as the site for Florida's capital.

Florida was kept off balance during much of the period by the Second Seminole War, the longest Indian war ever fought in this country. The Seminoles' lands, ceded them by treaty, were eventually seized by the U.S. Army, and they themselves were either killed, shipped to the trans-Mississippi West, or forced into exile in the Everglades. Altogether, it was one of the darkest chapters in Florida's long history.

Above: An undivided Florida became a possession of the United States in 1821. Andrew Jackson (1767–1845), hero of the War of 1812 and a future U.S. president, was appointed first governor. Jackson created Florida's first two counties, Escambia and St. Johns.

Right: The most celebrated figure to emerge from the Second Seminole War in Florida (1835–42) was Osceola, a half-breed (Creek and English) "Indian" from Alabama who became a war leader in the Seminole cause. Following his capture by the U.S. Army under treacherous circumstances, he was painted by artist George Catlin in 1838.

Florida became a U.S. territory in 1822 and retained
that status until becoming the twenty-seventh state
of the American Union in 1845. This seal was used for
official documents from 1838 to 1845. Five appointed
governors served in office during the territorial period. The first elected governor after statehood was
Jefferson County planter William D. Moseley.

These tabby slave quarter ruins remain from a cotton plantation founded in 1821 by Zephaniah Kingsley and his Senegalese wife Anna Madgigine Jai. Its location was on Fort George Island near the mouth of the St. Johns River. Kingsley would eventually own five plantations in northeast Florida.

6

I would name the periods of **early statehood**, **Civil War**, and **Reconstruction**. They were all a piece. With an ever enlarging population of immigrants from states to the north, particularly in the cotton growing counties, Florida was admitted to the Union as the twenty-seventh state on March 3, 1845. The first elected governor, Jefferson County planter William D. Moseley, took the oath of office in May of that year.

As a slave-holding state, however, only sixteen years later Florida seceded from the Union, the third southern state to do so. As a member of the Confederacy she sent 14,000 men to fight in what we now commonly call the Civil War. Union forces occupied most of Florida's port cities during the struggle, and only one major battle was fought here, at Olustee (near Lake City), on February 20, 1864. It was precipitated by a Federal push westward out of Jacksonville both to acquire raw materials and to cut off the Confederacy's supply of Florida beef and pork. An equal force of Confederates met the invaders, and, during a six-hour fight, forced the Union troops to withdraw.

A federally enforced Reconstruction period that followed the South's defeat in 1865 provided Florida's freed black population their first opportunities for education and participation in public life. A Freedmen's Bureau established by Congress organized black schools and orphanages. In a local initiative, the Roman Catholic bishop of Florida recruited nuns from France to teach black children in St. Augustine, Jacksonville, and three smaller towns. Among African Americans who earned political office at this time, one was elected three times to the U.S. House of Representatives, and another became Florida's secretary of state.

The lone major Civil War battle in Florida took place at Olustee, near Lake City, on February 20, 1864. Union troops marching west out of Jacksonville were met by a Confederate force at noon. The resulting action, lasting six hours, resulted in a Confederate victory.

After Florida seceded from the Union in 1861 artillery fire rang through Pensacola Bay. Union forces occupied Santa Rosa Island and Confederate troops manned fortifications on the mainland. Their respective artillery batteries twice exchanged fire. The cannon pictured here belonged to Confederate gunners at Fort Barrancas.

7

I would identify the years 1877 to 1920 as the **Flagler era**. Federal reconstruction troops withdrew from Florida in 1877, and the peninsular state became sharply divided between a white supremacist majority and an African American minority, who, by consequence of a gradually imposed program of Black Codes, Jim Crow laws, and poll taxes, lapsed back into a servitude in fact if not in law. By 1890 most blacks could no longer vote. Not until the second half of the twentieth century would their civil and social rights be restored.

The white population, meanwhile, prospered. By 1880 it had increased markedly in number. Sixty-four percent of residents had been born in the state, a figure never equaled afterward. Agriculture, particularly citrus groves and winter vegetables, took root in the central and southern counties, and tourism became a growth industry. Beginning in the 1870s various maritime entrepreneurs conducted tourist cruises on paddlewheel steamboats up and down Florida's interior rivers. The first to do so, it appears, was Hubbard Hart, who carried fifty thousand passengers a year on the Ocklawaha, one of America's most scenic rivers.

But the major force in launching the state's modern tourist industry, now Florida's largest revenue producer, was Standard Oil tycoon Henry Morrison Flagler. In 1888 he built the luxurious Ponce de Leon Hotel in St. Augustine, then constructed the Florida East Coast Railway south to Miami and Key West, building other resort hotels along the route.

Another railroad magnate of the time was Henry B. Plant, from Connecticut, who built the exotic Tampa Bay Hotel. His main Florida rail line joined the Gulf port of Tampa to the Atlantic port of Jacksonville.

Henry Morrison Flagler (1830–1913) became enchanted with St. Augustine on a honeymoon visit in 1883. He thought that, with his wealth, he could transform the state's Atlantic coast into an American Riviera. What was needed first, he decided, was a grand hotel at St. Augustine.

Flagler hired two young and relatively unknown Beaux-Arts architects, John M. Carrère and Thomas W. Hastings, to design this Spanish-Moorish fantasy, the Ponce de Leon Hotel, at St. Augustine. Regarded at its opening in 1888 as the most palatial hotel in the world, it is now the home of Flagler College. Carrère and Hastings went on to design Manhattan's famed Public Library on Fifth Avenue.

From St. Augustine Flagler constructed the Florida East Coast Railway south to the southernmost counties, building resort hotels along the route, such as the Royal Poinciana and The Breakers in Palm Beach and the Royal Palm in Miami. In a daring move he extended his line, as shown here, overseas to Key West.

8

I would propose the **1920s runaway land boom**. Nothing like it had been seen in the country before; not even the oil and free-land stampedes elsewhere matched it. In 1925 over two and a half million people came south into Florida, mainly to Dade County, looking for fifty feet in paradise. Miami, Coral Gables, Miami Beach, and other sites offered irresistible plea- sure domes to northern buyers, who made down payments on paper binders that in too many cases proved worthless. By 1926 the boom went bust and Florida entered the Great Depression three years ahead of the rest of the country. As Groucho Marx said about the land sales: "You can get stucco. Oh, how you can get stucco!"

As the Dixie Highway became black with automobiles heading back north, nature administered a coup de grace in the form of two Atlantic hurricanes, in 1926 and 1928, which caused appalling loss of life in Dade, Glades, and Palm Beach counties.

Still, at the close of the twenties, there were some encouraging signs: the state's population had increased by nearly half, and nine new counties had been created. With help from the federal government Florida successfully rode out the Great Depression during the decade that followed.

It should not escape notice that the twenties and thirties were decades when Florida women began to play an active and visible role in public life. A leader in the movement was May Mann Jennings, spouse of an early-twentieth-century governor. Whereas her gender had long been relegated to the nursery and kitchen, the hospital ward and classroom, May Mann called female citizens into the political arena where they fought, successfully, for such causes as women's suffrage, conservation of the natural environment, compulsory education, the Florida State Library, a State Park Service, and an Everglades National Park.

During the years 1920–26, 2.5 million people poured into Florida looking for homesites in what overwrought developers advertised as "an emerald kingdom lapt by southern seas." Here a real estate salesman on the back seat of his convertible bellows the virtues of his predevelopment scheme. Unfortunately, many such schemes proved fraudulent. Often homesites were sold before they were dredged above the water level.

In the wake of the land sales collapse, two devastating hurricanes hit the region of Dade, Broward, Glades, and Palm Beach counties, in 1926 and 1928. The first storm killed 392 residents and made 18,000 homeless. Some of the damage done to downtown Miami is shown in this photograph. The second storm killed 2,000, mostly black farm workers.

In 1926 the boom went bust: Paper binders on most of the property sold by hucksters (called "Binder Boys") turned out to be worthless. Some new homes survived the collapse, such as this stucco dwelling in De Soto county.

May Mann Jennings (1872–1963) was the first Florida woman to organize her gender in public and political activity. From 1914, when she became president of the Florida Federation of Women's Clubs, until her death five decades later, she was the most influential woman in the state. Her home was in Jacksonville but her presence was everywhere.

9

I would name the **second World War**, particularly the years 1942 to 1945. In an unexpected reprise of the twenties boom, 2.1–million service men and women poured into Florida for military training. The Army Air Forces alone occupied 70,000 hotel rooms on Miami Beach, where five acres of servicemen did calisthenics in gas masks, and an alert movie fan could catch sight of Clark Gable, William Holden, or Robert Preston in close order drill. The Army's Camp Blanding, near Starke, with 80,000 recruits and draftees, became Florida's fourth largest city, behind Jacksonville, Miami, and Tampa.

With Florida's good year-round flying weather and level terrain, the Army and Navy operated forty airfields from Pensacola to the Keys, including Eglin Air Proving Ground in the Panhandle where Lieutenant Colonel James H. Doolittle trained his B-25 bomber pilots for their surprise carrier-launched raid on Japan in 1942. Even before and during

U.S. entrance into the war British Royal Air Force cadets took flight training at Dorr and Carlstrom fields in Arcadia.

In June 1942 four German saboteurs came ashore from a submarine, or U-boat, near Ponte Vedra. Their bumbling operation was discovered and tracked by the Federal Bureau of Investigation. All four men were electrocuted by the U.S. Army two months after their landing. Far more serious were twenty-four U-boat torpedo attacks in Florida coastal waters against U.S. and Allied freighters and tankers. The sinking of those ships, which carried raw materials, oil, and aviation gasoline, was seriously damaging to the U.S. war effort. The torpedo explosions, the columns of smoke, and the debris swept onto shore brought the war visibly to the doorsteps of stunned beach-cottage residents.

With American entry into World War II, U.S. armed forces established training bases throughout the state. Army Air, Navy, and Marine pilots trained on forty Florida airfields. Camp Blanding, near Starke, became the nation's largest ground Army basic training center. In this photograph landing exercises take place at Carrabelle Beach in 1942.

From February to August, 1942, Florida's coastal sea lanes were infested by German U-boats (submarines). They preyed on U.S. and Allied freighters and tankers loaded with war cargoes. Of the twenty-four sinkings in Florida coastal waters, the most highly visible was the torpedoing of the tanker SS *Gulfamerica* off Jacksonville Beach. This photograph depicts a stricken tanker off Hobe Sound.

Army Air Force cadets march down a street in Miami Beach in 1943. One-fourth of all air officers and one-fifth of all air enlisted men took ground school in that resort city, occupying 70,000 hotel rooms. Hotels elsewhere also housed military trainees, including the Biltmore in Coral Gables, the Hollywood Beach, and the Ponce de Leon in St. Augustine.

Air training exercises in Florida took a terrible toll
during World War II. Of the Army's difficult-to-fly
B-26 medium bombers, taking off from MacDill Air
Base in Tampa, it was commonly said, "One-a-day
in Tampa Bay." Navy dive bomber pilots flying out
of DeLand, Vero Beach, and Fort Lauderdale in 1944
died at the rate of one-a-day. In this photograph
rear-seat gunner and Florida native Billy Willis flies
in No. 10 Navy aircraft over New Guinea in the
Pacific war.

Here, on July 7, 1944, the Tampa Shipbuilding & Engineering Company receives an Army-Navy award for wartime ship production. At Pensacola 7,000 workers, many of them women—"Rosies the welders"—were engaged in ship construction. Jacksonville was a prime contractor for merchant "liberty ships" and Navy torpedo boats.

10

Finally, I would name the three factors that, taken together, made possible the beginning of the post–World War II population increase that Florida has experienced as a continuous spiraling phenomenon from 1945 to the present. Those factors were: **air conditioning, mosquito control,** and **VA home loans.** Leading the boom were men and women who had trained in Florida, liked what they had seen, and, at war's end, returned to make Florida their home. From the 1950s forward, new residents, from seven hundred to a thousand per day, poured into Florida, those from the eastern seaboard states making their homes primarily in the Atlantic coast counties, those from the Midwest settling mainly in the Gulf Coast counties. Millions of other residents arrived from the Caribbean and from Central and South America.

In their attempt to serve those multitudes local and state governments were hard-pressed to provide a sufficient number of streets and highways, sewage systems, K–12 classrooms,

No complaint about Florida from Spanish times to the 1940s was more persistent than the complaint about mosquitoes. Along the Indian River, to take one example from the early 1940s, salt water mosquitoes were so thick residents could reach out and grab them by the handful. Only smudge pots and oil of citronella on the skin could ward them off. At war's end, Florida intensified chemical spraying. The state also reduced standing water breeding areas, as shown here in Dade County.

teachers, police officers, state prison beds, and, each day, 178 gallons of fresh water per person.

By 2006 the net population increase numbered 1,060 persons per day.

In just over fifty years Florida grew from its position as one of the least populated southern states to its present standing as fourth largest state in the Union. Where in 1880, 64 percent of Floridians had been born in the state, Florida is now reckoned as a place where everyone, it seems, is from somewhere else. Greater Miami, for example, is a major Hispanic/Latino center of banking, trade, and culture.

Among Florida's families we can find New Yorkers and Ohioans, African Americans, Seminole, Minorcans, Greeks, Italians, Poles, Finns, Danes, Haitians, African Bahamians, Syrian-Lebanese, Asians; and, of course, Canadians everywhere. Clearly, Florida today is a multicultural society with few parallels elsewhere.

The iconic political figure for such an inclusive state remains LeRoy Collins, of Tallahassee, who served as governor from 1955 to 1961. One of the founders of the "New South," Collins actively recruited business and industry to Florida; expanded higher education; and steered a moderate course in the integration crisis that followed the 1954 U.S. Supreme Court decision *Brown v. Board of Education*. Upon his death in 1991, the state house of representatives unanimously named him "Floridian of the Century."

TIME

THE WEEKLY NEWSMAGAZINE

**FLORIDA'S
GOVERNOR COLLINS**

Governor LeRoy Collins appeared on the cover of *TIME*, December 19, 1955. The national notice was recognition of the governor's successes in bringing non-smokestack industries into Florida, in improving public education at all levels, and in promoting year-round tourism. He soon would become all the more visible in the national media as the result of his courageous and moderate leadership of Floridians in the wake of the *Brown v. Board of Education* school desegregation order of the U.S. Supreme Court.

A major political event of the late 1960s was reapportionment of the state legislature on the basis of "one person, one vote." The action, long sought by the populous southern counties, broke the hammerlock that the rural northern counties had held on the legislative process. Overnight, Dade County's representation in Tallahassee increased from one senator and three representatives to nine senators and twenty-two representatives.

Democrats had long been the majority party in Florida, when, in 1967, Republican Claude R. Kirk Jr. broke the mold, becoming the first Republican governor since Reconstruction times. His surprising victory, made possible by the votes of many conservative Democrats, was a portent of things to come. A second Republican, former Tampa mayor Robert "Bob" Martinez, served a term as governor starting in 1986. During most of the last thirty years of the twentieth century Florida was governed by Democrat-dominated legislatures and by three Democrat governors in the Collins progressive tradition: Reubin Askew (1971–1979), Robert "Bob" Graham (1979–1986), and Lawton Chiles (1990–1998). In the legislative elections of 1996, however, the Republican party gained a majority in the state house of representatives; and, two years later, it won control of the state senate as well.

Complete command of state government passed into Republican hands in 1998, when John Ellis "Jeb" Bush, son of one president and brother of another, won the office of governor.

At Cape Canaveral, halfway down Florida's Atlantic shore, the federal government established a launching site for military and civilian rockets. The triangular-shaped cape, given its name by Spanish explorers in the early sixteenth century, provided a geophysical benefit from the earth's rotation as well as the proximity southeastward of tracking stations on the Caribbean Islands. Readers of Jules Verne's book *From the Earth to the Moon*, first published in 1865, had reason to recall that the French science fiction writer predicted that this particular latitude of Florida would be the launching site of humanity's first voyage to the moon.

On July 16, 1969, three American astronauts lifted off from the cape on a rocket flight called Apollo XI, and, four days later, two of them walked on the surface of the moon. During the next three years the cape launched five more lunar landings. In recent decades the cape has been the base for rocket-powered, reusable shuttles that have been engaged in the construction and maintenance of an international space station.

Apart from the space launching program, Florida is best known throughout the country and the world for its beaches and sunshine, its Disney World and cruise ships, its golf courses and retirement communities. But even Paradise has its problems, most notably the marring and fouling of Florida's semitropical environment. The storied Ocklawaha River was dammed, creating a 9,000-acre impoundment; the thin-sheeted and meandering Kissimmee River, which promoted

The first missile launched at Cape Canaveral was this WAC Bumper V-2, July 24, 1950. Toward the end of the decade, a newly created National Aeronautics and Space Administration (NASA) began placing satellites in space from the cape. Three manned projects in the 1960s, Mercury, Gemini, and Apollo, led to six human visits to the surface of the moon. The influx of NASA personnel and associated space industries has had an enormous impact on the populations and economies of Brevard and Orange counties.

rain cloud formation in the central counties, was canalized; and 50 percent of the wetlands in south Florida was obliterated by the Army Corps of Engineers. A newly vocal environmental movement has called for restoration, where it is still possible, of such degraded features of the original Florida.

In less visible ways the state's fragile ecosystems have been compromised by contaminants. By 1998 only one-half of Florida's lakes and waterways were found clean enough for recreation and fishing. Industrial and agricultural discharge of wastes, chemicals, and nutrients had been the primary offender; those violations have come under ever-tightening control by municipalities and counties. The principal remaining source of pollutants is real estate development: rain falling on streets, driveways, and lawns causes runoff of oil, fertilizers, and pesticides into nearby waterways.

Florida's freshwater springs, some 600 in number, are similarly threatened. Many are covered in part by green algae or hydrilla; others are polluted by nitrates; and still others are drying up as increasing amounts of groundwater are pumped out for use by cities, farms, and golf courses.

No feature of Florida's landscape has drawn more worried attention in recent years than has the dying Everglades. That unique "river of grass" which courses south from Lake Okeechobee to Florida Bay has been poisoned over the years by runoff of fertilizers and pesticides from the sugar plantations, winter vegetable fields, and dairy farms that border the

The Florida of today, nearing the 18-million mark in population, is projected soon to become the nation's third largest state, surpassing New York. Florida's numerous large cities exhibit gleaming new architecture, since most of their growth has been comparatively recent. Some of the most impressive urban architecture, however, dates from as far back as the 1930s, when streamlined Art Deco hotels rose from the sands of Miami Beach, a part of which is shown in this aerial view.

glades. In the year 2000 Congress passed a $7.8 billion measure to clean and restore both the water and the habitat for mammals, birds, amphibians, and reptiles. The rescue of that roadless wilderness, three-quarters the size of West Virginia, will take an estimated 38 years.

There are other problems, too, that Floridians have had to confront. Older citizens will remember the Cross Florida Barge Canal, the Mediterranean fruit fly, and the Mariel boat lift. Middle-aged citizens will recall cocaine cowboys, uncontrolled urban sprawl, and city commission corruptions. And young citizens will know about the state's low national ranking in expenditures per pupil in the K-12 years; about wretched ballots and voting machines; and about deadly hurricanes, six of which particularly afflicted Florida in the years 2004–5, leaving scores of residents and tourists dead, causing power outages, shortages of food, ice, and gas, and insured property damage in the billions of dollars.

If there is one benefit that has been garnered from those six punishing storms it would seem to be that they brought Floridians closer together in a semblance of statewide community. Florida has always been a fragmented society, owing to the independent nature of its eleven major cities, out-of-state birthplace loyalties, ethnic and race distinctions, marked age differences, and physical distances—the road distance from Key West to Pensacola, for example, is almost that from Pensacola to Chicago.

I like what Florida novelist Connie May Fowler wrote after the four hurricanes of 2004: ". . . Folks in Punta Gorda to the west, Stuart to the east, and Pensacola to the north grieve with one voice. We feel embattled, cursed, ravaged. Yet, still, we know we'll return to normal. It won't be the same normal that existed before Aug[ust] thirteen. It will be better. Perhaps this is my attempt to impose meaning on chaos," Ms. Fowler continued, "but I believe that because of our common experience with this hurricane season from hell, Floridians from tip to stern are finally thinking of themselves as one people and [of] this wild land as home."[1]

---

1 Fowler, Connie May, "Postcards From the Squalls," *New York Times*, October 3, 2004, 4.11.

Books on Florida History

The following select list of history titles will introduce the general reader to the wide array of books about Florida's past. Not all of these titles are still in print, though a surprisingly large number can be purchased through bookstores; but all are available in libraries and through interlibrary loan. Much of the literature about Florida history has appeared not in book form but in articles, as, for example, those in the *Florida Historical Quarterly*. Current and back issues of the *Quarterly* are available in most libraries. The reader should also inquire locally about regional historical journals and newsletters, such as *Tequesta: The Journal of the Historical Association of Southern Florida*; *Tampa Bay History*; *Gulf Coast Historical Review*; and *El Escribano: The St. Augustine Journal of History*.

GENERAL HISTORIES

Abbey, Kathryn Trimmer (Kathryn Hanna). *Florida, Land of Change*. Chapel Hill: University of North Carolina Press, 1941.

Colburn, David R., and Jane L. Landers, eds. *The African-American Heritage of Florida*. Gainesville: University Press of Florida, 1995.

Derr, Mark. *Some Kind of Paradise: A Chronicle of Man and the Land in Florida*. Reprint. Gainesville: University Press of Florida, 1997.

Douglas, Marjory Stoneman. *The Everglades: River of Grass*. Rev. ed. Miami: Banyan Books, 1978.

Gannon, Michael, ed. *The New History of Florida*. Gainesville: University Press of Florida, 1996.

Hoffman, Paul E. *Florida's Frontiers*. Bloomington: Indiana University Press, 2002.

Mormino, Gary R. *Land of Sunshine, State of Dreams: A Social History of Modern Florida*. Gainesville: University Press of Florida, 2005.

Tebeau, Charlton. *A History of Florida*. 1971. Rev. ed. Coral Gables: University of Miami Press, 1980.

Milanich, Jerald T., and Charles H. Fairbanks. *Florida Archaeology*. New York: Academic Press, 1980.

Milanich, Jerald T. *Florida's Indians from Ancient Times to the Present*. Gainesville: University Press of Florida, 2000.

Wright, J. Leitch, Jr. *The Only Land They Knew: The Tragic Story of the American Indians in the Old South*. New York: Free Press, 1981.

DISCOVERY AND EXPLORATION (1513–1565)

Milanich, Jerald T., and Charles Hudson. *Hernando de Soto and the Indians of Florida*. Gainesville: University Press of Florida, 1993.

Morison, Samuel Eliot. *The European Discovery of America: The Southern Voyages, A.D. 1492–1616*. New York: Oxford University Press, 1974.

Núñez Cabeza de Vaca, Alvar. *La "Relación" o "Naufragios" de Alvar Núñez Cabeza de Vaca*. Edited by Martin A. Favata and Jose B. Fernández. Potomac, Md.: Scripta Humanistica, 1986.

Sauer, Carl O. *Sixteenth-Century North America: The Land and the People as Seen by the Europeans*. Berkeley: University of California Press, 1971.

FIRST SPANISH PERIOD (1565–1763)

Bense, Judith A., ed. *Presidio Santa María de Galve: A Struggle for Survival in Colonial Spanish Pensacola*. Gainesville: University Press of Florida, 2003.

Bushnell, Amy Turner. *Situado and Sabana: Spain's Support System for the Presidio and Mission Provinces of Florida*. New York: American Museum of Natural History, 1994.

Deagan, Kathleen A. *Spanish St. Augustine: The Archaeology of a Colonial Creole Community*. New York: Academic Press, 1983.

Gannon, Michael V. *The Cross in the Sand: The Early Catholic Church in Florida, 1513–1870*. Gainesville: University of Florida Press, 1965, 1983.

Hann, John H. *Apalachee: The Land between the Rivers*. Gainesville: University of Florida Press, 1988.

Hann, John H. *A History of the Timucua Indians and Missions*. Gainesville: University Press of Florida, 1996.

Landers, Jane. *Black Society in Spanish Florida*. Urbana: University of Illinois Press, 1999.

Lyon, Eugene. *The Enterprise of Florida: Pedro Menéndez de Avilés and the*

Spanish Conquest of 1565–1568. Gainesville: University of Florida Press, 1976, 1983.

TePaske, John Jay. *The Governorship of Spanish Florida, 1700–1763*. Durham, N.C.: Duke University Press, 1964.

Weber, David J. *The Spanish Frontier in North America*. New Haven: Yale University Press, 1992.

Weddle, Robert S. *The Spanish Sea: The Gulf of Mexico in North American Discovery, 1500–1685*. College Station: Texas A&M University Press, 1985.

BRITISH FLORIDA (1763–1784)

Coker, William S., and Robert R. Rea, eds. *Anglo-Spanish Confrontation on the Gulf Coast during the American Revolution*. Pensacola, Fla.: Gulf Coast History and Humanities Conference, 1982.

Fabel, Robin F. A. *The Economy of British West Florida, 1763–1783*. Tuscaloosa: University of Alabama Press, 1988.

Schafer, Daniel L. *St. Augustine's British Years, 1763–1784*. St. Augustine: St. Augustine Historical Society, 2001.

Wright, J. Leitch, Jr. *Florida in the American Revolution*. Gainesville: University of Florida Press, 1975.

SECOND SPANISH PERIOD (1784–1821)

Coker, William S., and Thomas D. Watson. *Indian Traders of the Southeastern Spanish Borderlands: Panton, Leslie and Company and John Forbes and Company. 1783–1847*. Gainesville: University of Florida Press, 1986.

Cusick, James G. *The Other War of 1812: The Patriot War and the American Invasion of Spanish East Florida*. Gainesville: University Press of Florida, 2003.

Gordon, Elsbeth K. *Florida's Colonial Architectural Heritage*. Gainesville: University Press of Florida, 2002.

Patrick, Rembert W. *Florida Fiasco: Rampant Rebels on the Georgia-Florida Border, 1810–1815*. Athens: University of Georgia Press, 1954.

Tanner, Helen Hornbeck. *Zéspedes in East Florida, 1784–1790*. Coral Gables: University of Miami Press, 1963.

TERRITORIAL FLORIDA (1821–1845)

Doherty, Herbert J. *Richard Keith Call, Southern Unionist*. Gainesville: University of Florida Press, 1961.

Mahon, John K. *History of the Second Seminole War, 1835–1842.* Rev. ed. Gainesville: University of Florida Press, 1985.

Schafer, Daniel L. *Anna Madgigine Jai Kingsley: African Princess, Florida Slave, Plantation Slaveowner.* Gainesville: University Press of Florida, 2003.

Smith, Julia Floyd. *Slavery and Plantation Growth in Antebellum Florida, 1821–1860.* Gainesville: University of Florida Press, 1973.

Thompson, Arthur W. *Jacksonian Democracy on the Florida Frontier.* Gainesville: University of Florida Press, 1961.

STATEHOOD, CIVIL WAR, RECONSTRUCTION, AND GILDED AGE (1845–1900)

Ackerman, Joe A., Jr. *Florida Cowman: A History of Florida Cattle Raising.* Kissimmee: Florida Cattlemen's Association, 1976.

Akin, Edward N. *Flagler, Rockefeller Partner and Florida Baron.* Gainesville: University Press of Florida, 1992.

Graham, Thomas. *The Awakening of St. Augustine: The Anderson Family and the Oldest City, 1821–1924.* St. Augustine: St. Augustine Historical Society, 1978.

Johns, John E. *Florida during the Civil War.* Gainesville: University of Florida Press, 1963.

Nulty, William H. *Confederate Florida: The Road to Olustee.* Tuscaloosa: University of Alabama Press, 1990.

Peters, Thelma. *Lemon City: Pioneering on Biscayne Bay, 1850–1925.* Miami: Banyan Books, 1976.

Shofner, Jerrell. *Nor Is It Over Yet: Florida in the Era of Reconstruction, 1863–1877.* Gainesville: University of Florida Press, 1974.

Williamson, Edward C. *Florida Politics in the Gilded Age, 1877–1893.* Gainesville: University of Florida Press, 1976.

TWENTIETH AND TWENTY-FIRST CENTURIES

Colburn, David R. *Racial Change and Community Crisis: St. Augustine, Florida, 1877–1980.* Gainesville: University Press of Florida, 1991.

Dyckman, Martin A. *Floridian of His Century: The Courage of Governor LeRoy Collins.* Gainesville: University Press of Florida, 2006.

Faherty, William Barnaby. *Florida's Space Coast: The Impact of NASA on the Sunshine State.* Gainesville: University Press of Florida, 2002.

Flynt, Wayne. *Cracker Messiah: Governor Sidney J. Catts of Florida.* Baton Rouge: Louisiana State University Press, 1977.

Garbarino, Merwyn S. *Big Cypress, A Changing Seminole Community.* New York: Holt, Rinehart and Winston, 1972.

Kallina, Edward. *Claude Kirk and the Politics of Confrontation.* Gainesville: University Press of Florida, 1993.

Key, V[aldimer] O., Jr. *Southern Politics in State and Nation.* New York: Alfred A. Knopf, 1949.

McGovern, James R. *Anatomy of a Lynching: The Killing of Claude Neal.* Baton Rouge: Louisiana State University Press, 1982.

Mormino, Gary, and George E. Pozzetta. *The Immigrant World of Ybor City: Italians and Their Latin Neighbors in Tampa, 1885–1985.* Urbana: University of Illinois Press, 1987.

Nolan, David. *Fifty Feet in Paradise: The Booming of Florida.* San Diego, Calif.: Harcourt Brace Jovanovich, 1984.

Proctor, Samuel. *Napoleon Bonaparte Broward, Florida's Fighting Democrat.* Gainesville: University of Florida Press, 1950. Reprint: University Press of Florida, 1993.

Wall, Joseph Frazier. *Alfred I. du Pont: The Man and His Family.* New York: Oxford University Press, 1990.

Michael Gannon is distinguished service professor emeritus of history at the University of Florida. Among other honors, he has received a lifetime achievement award from the Florida Historical Society and the decoration Knight Commander of the Order of Isabel la Católica from King Juan Carlos I of Spain. He is author of *The Cross in the Sand: The Early Catholic Church in Florida, 1513–1870* (UPF, 1965, 1983), *Rebel Bishop: Augustin Verot, Florida's Civil War Prelate* (UPF, 1997), and the best-selling *Florida: A Short History* (UPF, 1993, 2003). He is the editor of *The New History of Florida* (UPF, 1996).

Related-interest titles from University Press of Florida

The African American Heritage of Florida
David R. Colburn and Jane L. Landers

Florida's Indians from Ancient Times to the Present
Jerald T. Milanich

Florida: A Short History, Revised Edition
Michael Gannon

Florida's Space Coast: The Impact of NASA on the Sunshine State
William Barnaby Faherty

Highway A1A: Florida at the Edge
Herbert L. Hiller

Land of Sunshine, State of Dreams: A Social History of Modern Florida
Gary R. Mormino

The New History of Florida
Edited by Michael Gannon

Some Kind of Paradise: A Chronicle of Man and the Land in Florida
Mark Derr

For more information on these and other books, visit our website at www.upf.com.